I Spy in the TEXAS SKY

Jack~

I Spy a
little Texan!
Keep looking up!
Enjoy.

Debby L.

I Spy in the TEXAS SKY

Written and Illustrated by
Deborah Ousley Kadair

PELICAN PUBLISHING COMPANY
GRETNA 2009

To my son Alexander, thanks for all the fun games of cloud and go seek
and for reminding me to keep looking up.
I Love You—Mom (DK)

The word "Pelican" and the depiction of a pelican are trademarks
of Pelican Publishing Company, Inc., and are registered in the
U.S. Patent and Trademark Office.

Library of Congress Cataloging-in-Publication Data

Kadair, Deborah Ousley.
  I spy in the Texas sky / written and illustrated by Deborah Ousley Kadair.
      p. cm.
  ISBN 978-1-58980-654-2 (hardcover : alk. paper) 1. Texas—Juvenile literature.
2. Guessing games—Juvenile literature. I. Title.
  F386.3.K33 2009
  976.4—dc22

                            2008040398

Printed in Singapore
Published by Pelican Publishing Company, Inc.
1000 Burmaster Street, Gretna, Louisiana 70053

I Spy in the TEXAS SKY

I spy in the Texas sky something familiar that's caught my eye.

It has long tail feathers, they're easy to see, and they make their home up in a tree.

Its colors are brown, gray, and white; when it needs to move, it just takes flight.

Can you guess what it is?

It is a MOCKINGBIRD (state bird)

The mockingbird was declared the state bird by the Texas Federation of Women's Clubs in 1927. They chose the mockingbird because it is found throughout the state, has a very distinct song, and is tenacious. The mockingbird is a fierce protector of its home, a characteristic shared with many a Texan!

I spy in the Texas sky something familiar that's caught my eye.

It graces fields across our state; its arrival in spring we celebrate.

With festivals, photos, and breathtaking views, one can't deny its beautiful blue hues.

Can you guess what it is?

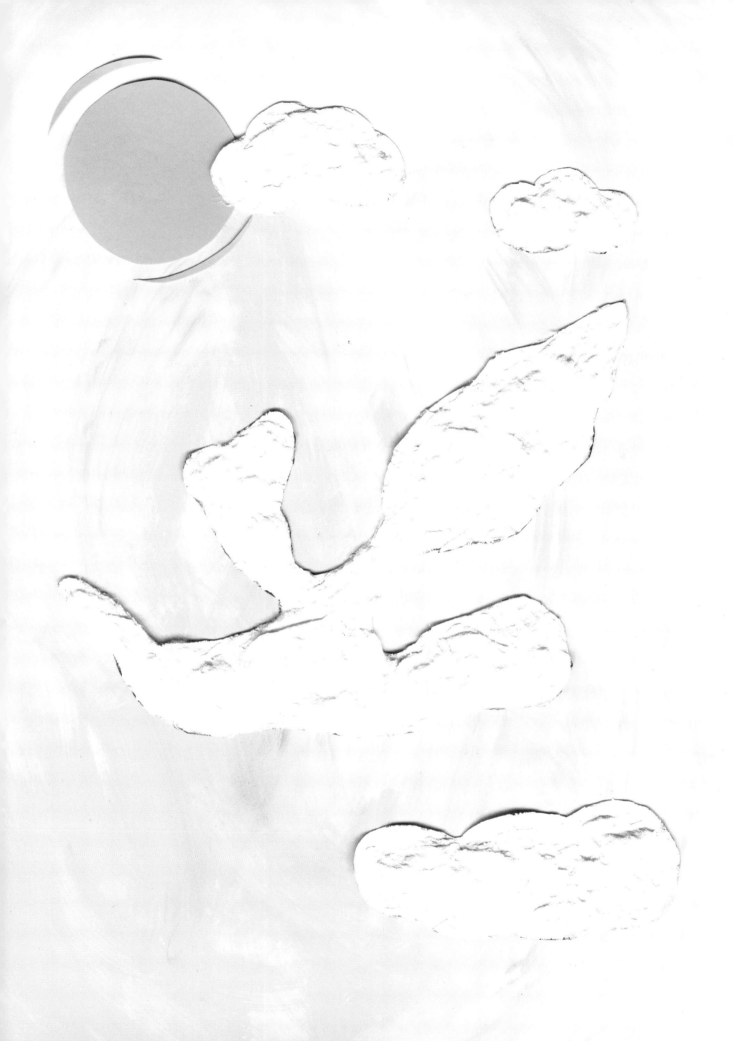

It is a BLUEBONNET (state flower)

The bluebonnet was adopted as the state flower of Texas in March of 1901. Because there are many types of bluebonnets that grow across various Texas regions, legislators voted in 1971 to include all of the indigenous species of bluebonnets to serve as the state flower.

I spy in the Texas sky something familiar that's caught my eye.

Spending its days turned upside down, under bridges is where its found.

When the sun goes down, it bursts into flight; when taking off, it's an awesome sight.

Can you guess what it is?

It is a MEXICAN FREE-TAILED BAT
(state flying mammal)

The Mexican free-tailed bat is a medium-sized bat that will grow to be about nine centimeters in size. They can be either dark brown or gray in color. The largest colony of free-tails reside under the Congress Avenue Bridge in Austin, Texas. The bats can be seen at dusk each night from mid March to late October when they migrate to Mexico.

I spy in the Texas sky something familiar that's caught my eye.

It can grow in rocky terrain; it is a plant that doesn't need much rain.

In the spring, it's sure to flower, but it also has amazing "poking" power.

Can you guess what it is?

It is a PRICKLY PEAR CACTUS
(state plant)

The prickly pear cactus can be found throughout the southwestern regions of the United States. They can grow in desert or rocky terrain and have very thick pads that are covered with spines. The blossoms of the prickly pear can be yellow, red, or purple.

I spy in the Texas sky something familiar that's caught my eye.

Hatching from eggs and eating vegetation, then transforming into a true fascination.

When its wings get strong, it's time to go; it migrates south to Mexico.

Can you guess what it is?

It is a MONARCH BUTTERFLY
(state insect)

The monarch butterfly was adopted as the state insect in 1995 at the urging of the students in District T, represented by Rep. Arlene Wohlgemuth. The monarch is the only butterfly that migrates as opposed to hibernation. These butterflies make their mass exodus every fall.

I spy in the Texas sky something familiar that's caught my eye.

It hides all day and scurries at night, digging for grubs before dawn's light.

Wearing armor wherever it goes, keeping it safe from would be foes.

Can you guess what it is?

It is an ARMADILLO (state small mammal)

In spite of the the armadillo's amour-type appearance, it is a mammal. The armadillo found in Texas is the nine-banded armadillo. These animals can grow to be 2½ feet long and will weigh between 12 and 17 pounds.

I spy in the Texas sky something familiar that's caught my eye.

Visible when the moon's a glow, for weary travelers the way it shows.

It's known best for its solitude, representing our state with a certain attitude.

Can you guess what it is?

It is the LONE STAR OF TEXAS
(great symbol of Texas)

The Lone Star is a symbol that has been used on flags in Texas since the 1830s. It made its first appearance on a flag used during a battle with Mexico. The Lone Star graces the Texas flag on a blue canton beside a dual-colored field. The colors of the field are white, which represents purity, and red, which represents bravery.